Insights Into the Mindset of Super Traders

Azeez Mustapha

ADVFN BOOKS

Contents

Introduction

This is a sequel to my two books, *Learn from the Generals of the Markets* and *What Super Traders Don't Want You to Know.*

"I know for myself: Study the pros in the area you are passionate in. You will inherit part of their killer instinct. Your brain will begin to mimic theirs. List the best. The ones you want to be like. Mimic them. List them every day. Think about what makes them win. You will develop a killer instinct. This is how I do it." – John Wallace, former star pro athlete

Speculation at first sight seems to be one of the easiest things in the world because you might think it's just making money by hitting the bid and ask buttons for the trading instruments of your choice. Hitting bid and ask buttons can be learned by everybody, but it remains a mystery that doing this does not bring easy money. It is no secret that the majority of traders lose. Pros know that. Newbies know that. Those who do not trade know that. Millions of trading styles and approaches have been used, but the majority of them seem not to be working.

Why?

The answer: you alone can determine whether you will become successful or not. Some want to succeed as traders but they get entangled in what can be called self-sabotage. They do exactly what looks satisfactory in the short-term, but which cannot help them in the long run.

What then is the way out?

You simply need to learn the insights, approaches and thoughts of super traders. And when you adapt and apply them to your trading styles, you will also find it easier to deal successfully with the vagaries of the market. That is when good strategies you use can work for you. Good strategies cannot work for you if you approach the market with illogical trading psychology.

Insights into the Mindset of Super Traders reveals the life stories of 20 selected master traders, how they think, how they view the markets, and how they make their fortunes.

The traders include:

- Lan Turner, who turns simple trading ideas into millions
- Dirk Vandycke, who has made thousands of percentage returns simply by accepting the truth about trading
- Michelle Williams, a female trader who once won a trading championship
- Martin Zweig, who was one of the most successful traders of the last century
- John Arnold, who became so rich that he retired himself at the age of 38, while many older people were still sweating over pensions
- Bruce Kovner, who is one of the least known billionaire traders
- Michael Platt, who is an accomplished trading risk manager
- Martin Schwartz, who lost money for nine years before becoming a permanently successful trader
- Louise Bacon, an old veteran trader who tells us his intriguing story
- Sir John Templeton, who is truthfully the greatest global stock picker of 20th century

There are many future master/pro/expert traders reading this book who are being discouraged by those who are ignorant of the realities in the market. They are being discouraged by temporary setbacks.

It doesn't have to be like this. The trading principles and insights contained in this book can help you become a wise trader, therefore helping you improve your trading results. You should take all the advice and instructions you can, so that you will be wise for the rest of your life.

Chapter 1

Lan Turner: Turning a Simple Trading Idea Into Millions

"Many would-be traders are afraid to take the profession seriously. They dream of making huge riches, but they aren't willing to put in the time and effort to make their dreams come true." – Joe Ross

Name: Lan Turner
Date of birth: 5 February 1964
Nationality: American
Website: Lanturner.com

Career

Lan Turner is a proficient public speaker, publisher and author. Being a professional trader in stocks, futures and Forex, he has more than two decades of experience in the financial industry. Lan is renowned for his seminars and trading ideas, having presented them in the US and other countries. He is the founder and CEO of Gecko. For many years, he taught finance at Utah State University. He designed Track 'n Trade and Trade Miner in 1998. He is also the president of PitNews Press and editor-in-chief of PitNews Magazine.

Insights

1. Success in other fields doesn't automatically translate to success in trading. Lan was successful as a distributor of computer hardware, and when he first invested his money in the markets, he made substantial gains. He thought he was good until he lost almost all the money. No matter your level of education or the kind of job you're doing, you still need to learn the art of trading because it's a different world entirely.

2. Gamblers lose their money right away or first gain money before they lose it all. When gamblers make money, they think they're good, just before the markets prove them wrong. Good traders may also lose money before they make money (or make money before they lose money) but they make gains and losses based on their trusted trading methods. In addition, the losses have minimal effects on their portfolios while the profits make their account grow; though not by leaps and bounds, but slowly and gradually.

3. When the going was tough, Lan didn't quit because he discovered he loved trading. You can't last long in the markets if you don't love trading with passion.

4. If you've become a success trader, how can you help others to become successful? How can you help others avoid the pitfalls that affected you badly in the past? Lan has found his secrets to success in the markets and he's doing his best to help others become successful through his products and services. His products and services are among the best in the trading industry. You can check his website in order to benefit from those products and services.

5. There are trading concepts and principles that work. You may already know some of them; others may come to you as a surprise. The knowledge you have is useless unless you use it to improve your life – hence your trading results. Lan Turner is an exponent of recurring trends and market cycles, which are genuine and powerful. For example, if you can know that USDJPY tends to rally within certain periods of every year, with about 80%, 90%, 95% or even 100% accuracy, for the past 10, 12, 14 or more years, you can take advantage of that knowledge. This is one simple idea that can be used to make millions/billions in the markets when used properly and applied to other trading instruments.

Conclusion

It's sensible to take the right position in the right market, otherwise things may not go as expected. Doing that is like being aware that a farmland is infested with rodents, yet still planting peanuts in it. We need trading methods that ensure everlasting safety of our portfolios. We want to take trades based on the seasonal trends that have proven dependable in the past. Although past results aren't indicative of future results, they can give us the best insight into the future. We wouldn't want to speculate based on the things that have proven to be flops in the past.

I end this chapter with a quote from Lan:

"If I only knew then, what I know now! Stop trying to reinvent the wheel, just use what works!"

Chapter 2

Dirk Vandycke:
Telling the Truth
about Trading

"All predictions are about the future. And, a lot of stuff can happen between now and then." – Dave Landry

Name: Dirk Vandycke
Country: Belgium
Profession: Trader, lecturer and software developer
Website: Chartmill.com

Career

Dirk Vandycke has been a trader and market researcher since 1995. He specializes in market dynamics, chart analysis and behavioural finance. He is a prolific writer (having written numerous insightful and helpful articles about trading) and a software developer. He also teaches software development and statistics at a Belgian University. Some of his though-provoking articles about trading can be found at: http://chartmill.com/documentation.php.

Insights

1. According to one writer, illusions are something very pleasant; the only disadvantage is that they tend to burst like a bubble. It is only illusion that makes us think that the secret to our success lies in trading strategies. Lies don't help people, otherwise the vast majority of traders wouldn't be losing. The truth about trading is blatant, yet that's what can help you. Many vendors tend to give you the impression that trading is easy. It isn't easy: you'll have to work hard before you reach a stage where you find it easier to make money.

2. When you get hold of a good strategy that has proven to be effective in the past, don't abandon it because of a losing streak. There's nothing in this world that isn't temporary – including losing streaks. Why would you abandon a great strategy when it's about to experience a winning streak again? If you abandon a good system because of a losing streak, the newly found system will also experience a losing streak sooner or later (or right away). You can't find lasting success by moving from one strategy to another. You can only find success by getting a positive expectancy system and sticking to it. You don't have any control over the movement of price, but you have control over your risk. You should lose as little as possible during a losing streak and

maximize your gains during a winning streak. By controlling your winners and losers, you'll end up being victorious and getting rewarded.

3. Software can really help in market analyses, thereby enabling us to make informed trading decisions. The software can help us scan the markets and filter out bogus setups, leaving us with great setups to choose from. This doesn't guarantee that the market will move in our favour. Nevertheless, the Golden Rule of trading will help us become triumphant. The Golden Rule has to do with cutting losses, running profits, managing money in a prudent way and rock-solid discipline.

4. Surprisingly, easy trading systems can generate better results when compared to intricate systems. Intricate systems aren't the Holy Grail, they just give more headaches when used to analyse the market.

Conclusion

There's no certainty in life. Why should you expect such in the markets? If there were certainty, then there would be no market. There's no guarantee that a person can't be sick. There's no guarantee that a person can still be alive by next month. There's no guarantee that a marriage can last for the next ten years. There's no guarantee that a person can retain her/his job for the next ten years. There's no guarantee that a student will get a good job immediately upon graduation. There's no guarantee that unforeseen times and events can't befall anybody. Why should we look for guarantees in trading? The uncertainty and the unpredictability that bring headaches, frustration and losses to some are the same factors that bring peace of mind, emotional and financial freedom to us. The unpredictability and uncertainty in the markets have become our friend. They're our ally, just as super traders have made them their ally.

This piece ends with a quote from Dirk:

"Don't focus on strategy, focus on the things we can control: cutting losses and riding (adding to) winners!"

Chapter 3

Michelle Williams: A Famous Daughter of a Famous Trader

"I was born with a fierce need for independence." – Michelle Williams

Name: Michelle Williams
Date of birth: 9 September 1980
Nationality: American
Profession: Actress

Career

Michelle is a popular actress, just as her father, Larry Williams is a popular trader. But although she is best known as an actress, she also has the pedigree of trading proficiency in her.

Michelle proved to be a true daughter of a great trader when she participated in the Robbins World Cup Championship of Futures Trading in 1997 and won the Cup by making 900% returns – making her the third highest winner of the Championship since its inception. Her father achieved the highest profit ever realized in the Championship, with 10,900% returns in a 12-month period.

As you might be aware, in 1987, Larry Williams was the winner of World Cup Championship of Futures Trading from the Robbins Trading Company. He turned $0.01 million to Over $1.1 million in twelve months.

Insights

1. It's possible to achieve good returns from trading. It's possible for women to achieve greatness as traders. It's possible for a man to be a great trader, and then for his children to be great traders, and then grandchildren, and then great grandchildren, etc. to be great traders. Trading excellence can become generational.

2. Doctors, lawyers, engineers, politicians, lecturers, scientists, accountants, artistes, actors, clerics, technicians, drivers, etc. (the list is endless) can become great traders. Michelle is a dedicated actress and a world trading champion.

3. Michelle felt a need for freedom at an early age. Therefore, she decided what she could do with her life when she was young. The need for freedom is an inborn tendency for humans, and financial freedom is part of that. Based on the quotes from Michelle, it's good to find your direction at an early age, so that you can

become successful while still relatively young. I've always reiterated the fact that it's good to start trading at an early age.

The quote at the top of the chapter is from Michelle and so is this one:

"I did find my direction at an early age."

Chapter 4

Martin Zweig:
One of the Most Successful
Traders of the Last Century

"It is easier to make money if you start with a good mentor: but mentors that make millions on their own and still accept to teach are really few in the industry." – Dr. Emilio Tomasini

Name: Martin Zweig
Date of Birth: 2 July 1942, Cleveland, Ohio
Nationality: American
Profession: Stock investor, investment adviser and financial analyst
Website: http://www.martinzweig.org/

Career

In 1964, Martin took his first degree at Florida Wharton School of the University of Pennsylvania. In 1967, he obtained an MBA from University of Miami, and after that he got a PhD in finance from Michigan State University. That was in 1969. He also taught finance at some colleges. Immediately after obtaining his PhD, he created a popular market indicator called the puts/call ratio. Using a combination of technical and fundamental analyses, he started writing articles and predictions about the markets in Barron's magazine.

He founded his own small-scale market newsletters, the Zweig Forecast. For many years, his articles and predictions were noticeably accurate and thus became popular. He appeared publicly on TV programs, and became more popular because of accurate timings of market movements. For example, on 16 October 1987, he predicted that the stock market would crash. On 19 October 1987, his prediction came to pass. No sooner had the oracle spoken than his prophecy came to pass. In 1986 he wrote a book titled *Winning on Wall Street*.

As a successful mutual funds manager, he was the chairman of Zweig-DiMenna Associates, Inc. Noted for his extravagant and lavish lifestyle; he owned the most expensive residence in the US at the time. In March 2013, the residence was worth $125 million. Towards the end of his life, he appeared less in public.

He died on 18 February 2013, on Fisher Island, Florida.

Insights

1. Martin's dream to become a great trader and a millionaire began in his early teenage years. He bought his first stock at age 13 and vowed to become a millionaire in life. Whatever your age may be, you can make a decision right now to become a profitable trader.

2. He was seriously inspired by a great trading legend – Jesse Livermore. He loved to read Edwin Lefèvre's book, *Reminiscences of a Stock Operator*, a book about Jesse Livermore. Martin's trading method was based on the inspiration he got from Jesse. His trading method also has some features that were similar to William O'Neil's highly successful CANSLIM investing method. Who is your role model? Who is the person that inspires you to greatness in trading?

3. His trading method combined technical and fundamental analysis, including certain characteristics of the markets he was interested in. The trading approach worked for him. In addition to this, he admitted that risk minimization and loss limitation are crucial to his trading method.

4. According to Martin, people somehow think you must buy at the bottom and sell at the top to be successful in the market. That's nonsense. The idea is to buy when the probability is greatest that the market is going to advance.

5. His book that was written in 1986, *Winning on Wall Street*, proved to be extremely helpful to investors who followed the advice in the book. They really won by following his trading ideas. As a result of this, he was featured in other books, like John Reese's *The Guru Investor: How to Beat the Market Using History's Best Investment Strategies*. Yes, if you're successful enough, people will write about you.

Conclusion

In order to be a success, you will need to understand what make people fail. To appreciate how to attain everlasting success, you need to learn how traders' careers can become short-lived. Many a person only wants to know how to become profitable in the markets, but you should be concerned about how to fail so that you can eventually avoid that and experience the opposite of failure. You should be aware of the factors that can kill your dreams as a trader and avoid those things like the plague.

This chapter concludes with a quote from Martin:

"I measure what's going on, and I adapt to it. I try to get my ego out of the way. The market is smarter than I am so I bend."

Chapter 5

Stanley Druckenmiller: Making Huge Killings in the Markets

"I had done alright at school and was regarded in my earlier profession as a clever and steady worker, but nothing of this was of any use in trading." – Tom Orton (Source: Trade2win.com)

Name: Stanley Druckenmiller
Country: USA
Date of birth: 14 June 1953
Profession: Super trader and philanthropist

Career

A son of a chemical engineer, Stanley Druckenmiller was born in Pittsburgh, Pennsylvania, USA, into a middle class family. He got his BA in English and Economics at Bowdoin College (1975). He started a PhD program in Economics at the University of Michigan, but he didn't finish the program because he was offered a job at Pittsburgh National Bank. He started his own company – Duquesne Capital Management – in 1981.

He also had some working experience in various capacities, including working for George Soros. He stopped working for Soros in 2000. He is featured in Jack Schwager's book titled *The New Market Wizards*.

In August 2010, he retired from trading public money when he closed his hedge fund, Duquesne Capital Management. He said that the constant effort to generate decent profits for his investors was taking a toll on his emotional health. He did so because he felt he wasn't making enough profits for his investors, for he thought that it was difficult to make profits when handling huge sums of money. Prior to this time, his fund was generating yearly profits of about 30% for 30 consecutive years, although there was a recent year in which a loss of only 5% was generated. Needless to say, the loss was recovered. By the time he closed his hedge fund, that fund was worth over $12 billion.

Undoubtedly, Stanley is one of the best funds managers to have ever lived on this planet. He received a salary of $260 million in 2008. At the time of writing this piece, Stanley was worth over $3 billion. He's a philanthropist who helps the causes he believes in.

Insights

1. Money shouldn't be your number one goal. Your number one goal should be trading mastery, though money is simply one of the rewards that will follow. Don't see trading as a means to get rich

quickly, but a means to improve a rare skill, a skill that will make you stand out of millions of people who simply sit down doing nothing, blaming others for their predicament. Speculation is one of the remaining doors to succeed in the present world of unequal opportunities and dismal economic situations. It's one of the rare opportunities that allows you to start with almost nothing and end up being rich in the end. But remember that money isn't everything. Even if you spend all your life chasing money, you can't be the richest person in the world, and you'll eventually discover that there are other things in life that are more important than money. So you need a balanced view of trading. There are other ways to attain happiness apart from one's net worth. Having money without these essential qualities in life will make you a miserable millionaire/billionaire.

2. Sure, it's possible to attain success in the markets. Stanley's compound returns of 30% per annum for 30 years are an evidence of this fact. Wise people agree with this fact and see the hypothesis of the efficient market as rubbish. We aren't saying that success is easy, but we say that it's possible despite the fact that it's hard to achieve and sustain. Traders who believe in the efficient market are indeed failures and losing traders who have given up. They simply use efficient market theory to justify their permanent failure. Yale professor Robert J. Shiller concluded that the efficient market hypothesis is one of the most remarkable errors in the history of economic thought. Really, many known and unknown traders have been making consistent profits for decades. Success needs conscientiousness and diligence. Nothing good comes easily. For you to become a successful trader, you need to work hard. Stanley Druckenmiller admitted that he worked hard, for the markets took much of his time, resources and energy. You just need to continue to work hard at doing the right thing so that you can stay on top of the game.

3. Success in life requires serious effort and doggedness. You can't be a successful market speculator if you hate trading. The love you have for the market will surely give you an advantage over those who hate the market. After much hard work, you'll find trading easier, more rewarding, fulfilling, exciting and life transforming.

4. Stanley likes to use a top-down approach when speculating, doing so conscientiously. Don't trade or continue trading when you're feeling bad. Good mood has a big role to play in your success. Stanley stopped managing other people's money when he felt he could no longer deliver. That doesn't mean he stopped trading, for he's still managing his own money privately.

5. It's a good thing for you to know how to change your mind when a position isn't going as envisaged. Cut your loss. You may be correct about your prediction and still lose money. You see, doing the right thing doesn't always make you look smart in the short term.

6. When you know there's no reason not to enter a trade (all your entry criteria have been met), trade with confidence. When you're right in your prediction, try to maximize your gain from the opportunity.

7. Position sizing is important in trading. This is the biggest determinant of the magnitude of your profits and losses, plus whether your objectives will be met.

Conclusion

We stay on in the game of speculation because we love it – just as some professionals in other fields of human endeavours. Those who love their calling don't retire until some circumstances beyond their control force them to do so.

This piece concludes with a quote from Stanley:

"The way to build long-term returns is through preservation of capital and home runs."

Chapter 6

Seth Klarman:
A Winner on Wall Street

"Value investing requires a great deal of hard work, unusually strict discipline, and a long-term investment horizon. Few are willing and able to devote sufficient time and effort to become value investors, and only a fraction of those have the proper mind-set to succeed."

Name: Seth Klarman
Date of Birth: 21 May 1957
Nationality: American
Profession: Value investor, funds manager, financier and philanthropist

Career

Belonging to the Jewish ethnicity, Seth was born and raised in the US. He worked for Max Heine and Michael Price, which is now part of Franklin Templeton Investments. In 1982, he founded Baupost Group and the firm grew and grew. Recently, it was estimated that the firm was managing more than $22 billion. He also authored a book titled *Margin of Safety: Risk-Averse Value Investing Strategies for the Thoughtful Investor.* That book – now out of print – is seen as a value investing classic.

In 2013, he earned an income of $350 million and subsequently he was named among the highest earning funds manager. As of 2014, he was worth $1.3 billion. Sometimes they call him the Warren Buffett of his generation.

Seth is involved in philanthropy and politics, heavily donating to the causes he believes in. He lives in Brookline, Massachusetts, and is married to Beth Klarman.

Insights

1. Seth makes great returns on his investments despite his unconventional investment methods. Sometimes he makes up to 50% per annum, by investing in unpopular instruments and looking for undervalued markets. You don't need to do what most others are doing in order to make money in the markets. No matter how odd your strategies are, they're OK as long as you make consistent gains. Let people criticize you. Let them say your trading style is weird; you're fine as long as it works for you.

2. You don't need to be a star or a celebrity before you can make money as a trader. There are many people who make money in their private living rooms without the public knowing. In certain cases, most of the so-called professionals who speak at seminars, trading shows, public events and on radio/television programs

aren't successful traders. Some of the loudest mouths are flops in the markets. As for Seth, he doesn't always speak in public and doesn't usually grant interviews, He keeps a low profile, despite being a market wizard.

3. The public don't know when the markets are overbought or oversold and that's why their timing tends to be wrong. For those who know how to play the markets, outperformance is possible.

4. According to Seth, successful investors tend to be unemotional, allowing the greed and fear of others to play into their hands. By having confidence in their own analysis and judgment, they respond to market forces not with blind emotion but with calculated reason. Successful investors, for example, demonstrate caution in frothy markets and steadfast conviction in panicky ones. Indeed, the very way an investor views the market and its price fluctuations is a key factor in his or her ultimate investment success or failure.

5. Some investors think of buying alone, though at times, it's better to bet on long-term bearish trend with some success. When one pays too much attention to the possibility of stocks going up without thinking of the possibility of the stocks going down, one may easily miss trading opportunities on the downside.

6. People invariably showcase their inability to profit from long-term investments based on real fundamental figures. Value investing is inherently long term in nature.

7. Computer programs and mathematics can do little to help you in the markets. In the end, you'd need to use common sense when handling investments. Unlike many people, think about how you can lose and try to control that. Don't think only of how much you can gain.

8. We like to look for simple solutions to intricate challenges: seeking success formulas. Searching for the Holy Grail is common, but that doesn't exist.

9. Remember what happened to CHF Pairs on 15 January 2015 (known as the Forex Black Thursday). When analysts express too much confidence in certain markets, you need to be very careful.

The quote above is from Seth Klarman and so is this quote one.

"Investors must try to understand the institutional investment mentality for two reasons. First institutions dominate financial market trading; investors who are ignorant of institutional behavior are likely to be periodically trampled. Second, ample investment opportunities may exist in the securities that are excluded from consideration by most institutional investors. Picking through the crumbs left by the investment elephants can be rewarding. Investing without understanding the behavior of institutional investors is like driving in a foreign land without a map. You may eventually get where you are going, but the trip will certainly take longer, and you risk getting lost along the way."

Chapter 7

Sam Zell:
A Famed Investor

"I appreciate the opportunity to manage money for others. A lot of people don't enjoy it, but I do." – Mike Melissinos

Name: Sam Zell
Date of Birth: 27 September 1941
Nationality: American
Occupation: Business magnate, investor and philanthropist
Website: www.egizell.com

Career

Sam's parents were Jewish immigrants who left Poland to settle in the States before the outbreak of the World War II. Sam was born in Chicago and he attended Highland Park High School in Highland Park, Illinois. He obtained a BA from the University of Michigan and later, he obtained a JD (Juris Doctor) from the University of Michigan Law School.

In 1967, Sam founded Equity Group Investments. Robert H. Lurie joined him and they worked together to transform the firm into a vast business empire. Lurie died in 1990, but the business continues to grow and grow and grow. One source confirms that the majority of Sam Zell's investment portfolio ranges across industries such as energy, logistics, communications and transportation, but he is often best known for his pioneering role and stewardship in creating the modern commercial real estate industry. Moreover, EGI's holdings also include fixed-income investments in public and private companies.

Sam is involved in various international and local causes, donating generously to them, including education. He has three children.

As of January 2015, Sam was worth about $4,900,000,000.

Insights

1. Good traders and investors are able to tackle the uncertainties in the markets, solving the problems of the unpredictable nature of the markets in simple ways. That's the secret of our ongoing success. We make complex problems (that put off people from the markets) look simple. We simplify these problems and come with simple solutions. That's exactly what Sam has been doing in decades – unravelling the mystery of various markets and amassing huge wealth by doing so.

2. There's one though-provoking quote on Egizell.com, which says: "Solid business strategy is not anchored in suit, or a tie. It comes from the gut. Corporate culture can't be dictated. It comes from the soul. A great company comes from the heart." How true that is!

3. The qualities of a good trader aren't measured by her/his attitude when things go right, when things are fine, and during winning streaks; but when the road is rough, tough and during losing streaks.

Conclusion

Winning strategies are the ones that go contrary to the expectation of the public, and that's why it takes serious discipline to follow such strategies. We want to follow good strategies when they work and when they don't work.

This chapter concludes with a quote from Sam:

"The reality is that I need to be challenged and interested, as long as the risk and reward is in line."

Chapter 8

Marc Rivalland:
Do You Know His Trading
Achievements?

"To be successful in the markets, you need to control your emotions and only act rationally. Since we never learned this in school, 90% of the traders and 80% of the investors are losing money." – Florian Grummes

Name: Marc Rivalland
Nationality: South Africa, the United Kingdom
Occupation: Lawyer, trader and author
Trading style: Swing trading

Career

Marc, who comes from South Africa, is a popular trader. He obtained a Bachelor of Commerce in 1975, and then worked as a market analyst in South Africa. He also studied law and settled in the UK. He continues working in various capacities in the financial industry, while also practicing law. He's developed his own speculation approaches with some measure of success. He has written a book on swing trading titled *Marc Rivalland on Swing Trading* and he has contributed a lot to trading journalism.

He currently lives in London, UK.

Insights

1. In order to take control of your destiny in the market, you need to be proactive. There's always something you can do when you see a signal, when your position is positive and when your position is negative.

2. Swing trading, like other trading styles, works. Many people become swing traders without knowing what it takes to be a successful swing trader. Marc has modified something called Gann swing charts – a tool that makes swing trading more profitable. Another useful tool is point and figure, which charts have been in use for more than a century. Marc, in addition, discusses some useful trading strategies, including the one that uses the RSI indicator. Each strategy discussed has its benefits (plus the downside isn't hidden). Many a strategy vendor tells people about the advantages of the strategies they're selling, while glossing over the disadvantages of those strategies. There's no perfect strategy and there won't be. The things we can do are good RRR, etc. Marc Rivalland mentions this fact in the quote at the end of this piece.

3. Even some professional traders can't have consecutively positive years indefinitely. Some years may have more profits than others, and some years may even be breakeven or negative years. In 2005, Marc experienced losses but he was able to recover the losses before the end of that year, ending at a breakeven. You may think he didn't make a profit, but we appreciate the fact that he was able to keep his money safe (which is the most important goal in trading). In the same year, another super trader named John Henry lost 11% (which he called a bad year for him). 11% loss is still better than 21% loss or 41% loss or 60% loss or even a margin call. The smaller a loss is, the easier it is to recover. Let this be a lesson. We take only what the market offers us and we're appreciative for that.

4. A trading approach that takes your time 24/7 or 24/5 is not an approach that really makes you free, irrespective of how much you earn. Trading brings freedom only when you spend minimal time and you still make money. Marc recently said this: "*I needed such a system that allowed me to place my orders, along with the stops and limits, with my broker at 7:55 in the morning and then work all day and not have to look at the market again until the close at 4:30 in the afternoon. In the evening I came home with the stock markets closed by then and my trades having been made. And that worked well. Over time, I shifted my focus to trading and also incorporated discretionary components.*" (Quote source: TRADERS' December 2012)

I conclude this chapter with a quote from Marc:

"*Overall, traders should make an effort to win the largest possible amounts in their profitable trades and only have small losing trades.*"

Chapter 9

Larry Hite:
What Can You Learn
from Him?

"The best strategy loses its effectiveness when you trade from a place of fear." —
Mercedes Oestermann van Essen

Name: Lawrence D. Hite
Nationality: American
Profession: Funds manager, trading systems developer, philanthropist

Career

Larry Hite is an award-winning funds manager who is one of the forefathers of trading strategies. In 1981 he co-founded Mint Investments, and several years later the firm became the most successful of its kind (at that time).

He was featured in Jack Schwager's book titled *Market Wizards*. Larry also partnered with Man Group and started some ground-breaking trading concepts – which also proved successful. In 2000, Larry shifted gears and focused on other things that also mattered to him, including family, investing, funds management and philanthropy. For instance, he founded his own foundation, called The Hite Foundation, which he heads. One source says he also serves as chairman of the Development Committee for the Institute of International Education's Scholar Rescue Fund, whose goal is to provide safe haven for academics and professionals who are at risk throughout the world.

Insights

1. No matter how great your trading method or analysis is, no matter how much information or knowledge you have, you can open a position and still experience negativity. Always see a new trade as a potential loser. Don't think of how much you can make, but think of how much you can actually lose. With that mindset, you'll risk as low as possible and trade defensively, thus ensuring your safety. What you can determine is how much you'll lose; you can't determine how much you'll gain.

2. Protect your wealth. Protect your capital. You need capital to play the markets, and without playing the markets, you can't make money. Without your capital, you can't play the markets, and that's why you need to protect your capital.

3. When you have a good system, please be faithful to it. It can't work always, but try not to deviate from it. Make this a hard-and-fast rule.

4. Always respect the market; otherwise, you'll suffer for your stubbornness. Go with the flow.

5. Larry says this: "I have a cousin who turned $5,000 into $100,000 in the option market. One day I asked him, 'How did you do it?' He answered, 'It is very easy. I buy an option and if it goes up, I stay in, but if it goes down, I don't get out until I am at least even.' I told him, 'Look, I trade for a living, and I can tell you that strategy is just not going to work in the long run.' In his next trade he put his money in Merrill Lynch options, only this time, it goes down, and down, and down. It wiped him out." Lesson: Simply cut your loss. Never allow it to run.

6. What you call markets are really risks, rewards, money and means to financial freedom. When risks are controlled and the flow of the markets is respected, things will work for you as traders.

7. Many speculators may have different kinds of stories to tell, but the truth is that we're all speculators. We're the same. We all have access to a level playing field.

Conclusion

All challenges we face in trading have their hidden blessings; but we're often blind to the blessings and allow disappointment, ire and fear to take control of our lives when a position doesn't do what we want it to do. One expert advises that trading should be treated as another splendid opportunity to learn something and improve our skill. We shouldn't concentrate on money alone.

This chapter ends with two quotes from Larry:

"There are just four kinds of bets. There are good bets, bad bets, bets that you win, and bets that you lose. Winning a bad bet can be the most dangerous outcome of all, because a success of that kind can encourage you to take more bad bets in the future, when the odds will be running against you. You can also lose a good bet, no matter how sound the underlying proposition, but if you keep placing good bets, over time, the law of averages will be working for you."

"I met the guy who wrote this best seller now called, Bringing Down the House, *it's about these MIT guys who beat the blackjack tables. And part of the problem, if you're going to be a blackjack counter is that the casinos don't like you. They actively don't like you. And they come and tell you in rather strong things to take your business away. Well, the beautiful thing about the markets, they don't like you, they don't dislike you, they just don't care. They are there every day. You want to play, you can play."*

Chapter 10

John Arnold: A Retired Natural Gas Trading King

"Negativity is real, but consistent loss is optional." – A.M.

Name: John Arnold
Year of birth: 1974
Nationality: American
Profession: Retired funds manager, investor and currently a philanthropist

Career

Raised in an upper-class home, in Texas, USA, John's father was an attorney and his mom was an accountant. While John was still a teenager, his father died. In 1995, he earned a Bachelor's degree in Economics and Mathematics from Vanderbilt University.

He started a great career at Enron, enjoying rapid promotion, owing to his ability to make huge profits for the company. There was a year in which he made $0.75 billion for his company and as a result, he was given $8 million as a bonus in that year. Since then, some people have called him 'king of natural gas trading.'

After Enron folded in 2002, John started his own firm with his bonus money. The firm, named Centaurus Advisors, LLC, became rapidly successful. Its assets grew to over $3 billion and it attracted some of the best traders around. The firm was based in Houston and it specialized in trading energy products. That was John's edge.

At the age of 38, John suddenly announced his retirement from active funds management. At least, he's extremely rich, for he's invested a lot. He's now doing what he also enjoys – philanthropy – donating to various interesting causes. John has touched many lives through his generosity and many more lives would be touched. As of March 2013, he was worth $2.8 billion. He is married to Laura Muñoz and they have three children.

Insights

1. Some enter the trading world because they are in pitiful situations and they want to get out. There are also some people like John, who are not from poor families. They enter the world of trading because they like the challenge and become richer than they ever thought could be possible.

2. John started his trading career while young, and he became a billionaire while still young. He retired in his late 30s. This

emphasizes the fact that it's better to start trading while young. John retired at the age of 38, but he continues to get richer because of his investments. He's now engaged in activities that he likes. Are you working to survive, or are you really engaged in what you like doing, and as a result have become financially free? You can retire any time you like, either early like John Arnold, or late like Stanley Druckenmiller.

3. You should continue to make progress, irrespective of peoples' criticisms. Some people now criticize John for what he currently does; yet he does what he thinks is right.

4. One of John's secrets is that he specialized in what he could do best. If he tried other things, he might not be as successful as he is. Some people lose money as stock traders, while making money with futures. Some people lose money with options but make money with Forex. Some people lose money trading popular majors but make money trading exotic pairs. Some people make money with discretionary approaches but lose money with mechanical approaches, and vice versa. Please find out what markets/trading instruments work for you and stick to it.

5. It's true that the market is risky, but continual losses are only a matter of choice. You can stop losing in the market if you want.

6. Look at his quote below, John liked to buy at troughs and sell at peaks: with great success. Please think about that.

This chapter is concluded with a quote from John:

"I try to buy things whenever they're trading below what [our] analysis shows to be fair value and sell things whenever our analysis shows that the forward curve is higher than our analysis of fair value."

Chapter 11

Bruce Kovner:
One of the Least Known
Billionaire Traders

"The biggest risk in trading is hubris… This is because being wrong is actually an integral part of success. A successful futures trader makes many more losing trades than winning ones. The key is to recognize and concede the mistakes and cut losses. And ride the winners." – Bruce Kovner

Name: Bruce Kovner
Date of birth: 25 February 1945
Nationality: American
Website: Caxton.com

Career

Born in New York, Bruce is from Jewish ethnicity. His family came from Czarist Russia, fleeing persecution for their political and religious beliefs.

He loved football and piano. He went to Harvard for a PhD program but he was unable to finish the program.

Following that, he tried a number of jobs, like playing harpsichord, writing and driving a taxi. He discovered trading as a career shortly after his first marriage (he has been married twice). He began trading in 1977 with a borrowed $3,000 and ended up making $23,000 with it. During the volatility the position was exposed to, the open profit even went up as high as $40,000. This made Bruce fall on love with the markets.

He worked under Michael Marcus – one of the trading geniuses featured in my previous books – and soon gained respect as a disciplined and reality-based trader. Eventually he founded his own firm, Caxton Associates, LP. The firm became so successful and managed around $14 billion at the apogee of their achievements.

Outside trading, Bruce Kovner isn't well known, for he seldom grants interviews and loves privacy so much. One source says that his Fifth Avenue mansion in New York City, the Willard D. Straight House, features a lead-lined room to protect against a chemical, biological, or dirty bomb attack.

He no longer works as CEO of his firm: he has retired from that position.

As of March 2015, Bruce was worth $5 billion. He is an active philanthropist and is also engaged in other interesting activities.

Insights

1. Bruce probably wouldn't make billions of dollars as a writer, or as a harpsichord player or as a cab driver. Or can you tell me of anyone who makes billions driving a cab? He was very lucky to

discover trading. You're very lucky to be reading this book. Few jobs can be as high paying as trading. Imagine someone who started trading with $3,000 in 1977 and is currently worth $5,000,000,000. That's Bruce Kovner. What can you learn from this?

2. Trading success will, undoubtedly, cost you hard work and unrelenting desperate effort to achieve trading mastery. Without accepting this reality, you can't be a good trader. Anyone telling you otherwise is a liar (and your experiences will later confirm this fact).

3. There's one thing that can't be avoided in trading: you must make mistakes constantly and learn from them. That's normal. You make a trading decision and lose. You repeat that and lose. You repeat that and lose. You make another trading decision and lose. Then a good winning period comes out and you recover the loss and move ahead. In time, your proficiency increases as you make fewer mistakes (which is defined as not following your rules).

4. Don't follow the masses, for they're always wrong. When most traders move in one direction, then the trend is about to change. If the masses were always right, most traders would be rich. But this isn't so. For example, there will soon be a breakout after most traders have noticed an equilibrium phase.

5. Short rallies in bear markets and the other way round for bull markets.

6. Bruce said risk management is the most important thing you need to understand. Undertrade, undertrade, undertrade is his second piece of advice. Whatever you think your position ought to be, cut it at least in half.

This chapter concludes with a quote from Bruce:

"My experience with novice traders is that they trade three to five times too big. They are taking 5 to 10 percent risks on a trade when they should be taking 1 to 2 percent risks. The emotional burden of trading is substantial; on any given day, I could lose millions of dollars. If you personalize these losses, you can't trade."

Chapter 12

Michael Platt:
One of the Most Effective
Risk Managers

"I am actually trading because I learn a lot of important life lessons from it. Trading helps me get to know myself. It helps me think about why I believe things and why I do things." – Van Eekelen

Name: Michael Platt
Date of Birth: 12 December 1968
Nationality: British
Occupation: Hedge fund titan

Career

Born in Preston, England, Michael attended the London School of Economics and earned a BSc with Honours. He was influenced by his grannie who was an investor. With the help of his grannie, he got his feet wet and was hooked. He began working at JP Morgan in 1991, being a managing director in charge of value investing. He took advantage of challenges and opportunities he encountered at JP Morgan.

He co-founded BlueCrest Capital Management LLP in 2000, and that firm is now Europe's third biggest hedge fund company. The firm manages over £30 billion and has 350 employees. They mainly employ systematic trading approaches, using computer programs to facilitate the approaches.

As of April 2015, Michael was worth £1.5 billion ($3.5 billion). He is married and currently lives in Geneva, Switzerland. He is an avid lover of arts and paintings.

Insights

1. When you make useful decisions in life, including trading, you'll simply end up having enough. You won't need to be striving after money. Then you will see trading as an interesting activity, not an onerous task. At the end, you'll be so rich to the extent that big money would not matter so much to you. For example, Michael Platt has become so rich to the extent that he once turned down an offer from George Soros. The latter wanted him to manage more than $1 billion for a 0.5% management fee and a 10% performance fee. But Michael said his investors were willing to pay management fees of 2% and performance fee of 20%. Many desperate professionals would jump at such an offer.

2. Please see the quote at the bottom of this chapter. Risk control is extremely important for your everlasting career as a trader. That's

your life insurance. Michael acknowledges that risk management is the most important thing. In bear markets, many funds crashed and burned, especially when they faced credit crunches in 2008. Yet Michael finished the year with 6%. He avoided loss and even made a small profit. What do you want those who lost to say?

3. Hear! Hear! Gamblers who think it's stupid to risk less than 1% per trade. Risk control is something that must be enforced in trading. One of BlueCrest's secrets is to make sure that each of their traders doesn't go below 3% drawdown, or they're deprived of 50% of the portfolio they manage. Another drawdown of 3% (making a total of 6%) would result in a trader getting their entire portfolio allocation removed. They may even lose their job if it's found that their trading method is suicidal. I currently risk 0.25% of my account per trade, and so I'll need to lose 12 trades in a row before I can go down 3%. This is a good plan for survival.

4. Many so-called professionals out there give advice that helps others make money, but not themselves. Ideas from professionals are valuable in that you can make profits from them, before the professionals themselves do so (they may not even do so). You can really take advantage of comments that are made by those trading professionals.

5. There are winning strategies, and you need to find one of those so that you can attain ultimate financial freedom, as a result of consistent profits in the markets. BlueCrest Capital International fund hasn't had a negative year since it was started – though some years were better than others. For example, the fund made a profit of 41% in 2009, earning hundreds of millions of dollars in fees only.

6. Leda Braga, featured in one of my past books, is a partner of Michael at BlueCrest. She manages a fund named BlueTrend. She is a pro trader, and she has been a blessing to BlueCrest. Great

minds think alike, for like will attract like. Do you have a good trader as a partner?

7. Success attracts more success. The more successful you are, the more investors you'll attract and the richer you're going to be. Because BlueCrest made a profit of $4 billion in 2008, they received about $5 billion in additional investment. But know this: the more you fail, the more investors you lose and the poorer you become. So you must know what you're doing.

8. Michael bets his own money alongside his investors. What a good trading idea! One trading specialist once advised that if funds managers' money is tied to the portfolios they manage, there wouldn't be rogue traders. When someone trades a fund which belongs entirely to her/his clients, they may be tempted to be careless because it's not their money.

9. Who encouraged you to become a trader? You should be forever grateful to such a person irrespective of what you're currently facing as a trader. The advice to start trading is really a billion-dollar advice. Michael was inspired and encouraged by his late grannie, and he is now a billionaire. I'm forever grateful to my uncle who advised me to become a trader.

10. Michael's father was an engineer, and so Michael wanted to study engineering. Suddenly, he changed his mind and studied economics instead. This prepared him for the task ahead. Engineers can also become successful speculators; albeit the lesson is that one does not always need to take up a career one's father loves, especially if one doesn't like the career.

11. Michael started small and now he is bigger. Please learn from this. When your performance is good, you'll enjoy so much success in a relatively short period of time. Michael's firm is now perceived with a higher level of credibility, even more than those who

started the fund management business before them. That's really an ideal achievement. Learn from that please.

Conclusion:

A judicious trader doesn't act on impulses, whatever they may be. According to Joe Ross of Tradingeducators.com, from a purely physical standpoint, it is essential to minimize the potential impact that a losing trade may have on your account balance. If you lose a lot on a single trade, it will sting. But if you limit the amount of capital you risk on a single trade, it won't hurt at all. You can pick yourself up easily and put on the next trade. It's much easier to take a loss in your stride when the real impact on your account balance is minimal.

This chapter concludes with a quote from Michael. Please think about it. Safety first!

"I've never hit the 3 percent drawdown… Ego is how you lose money in this business. I put a trade on, and if it doesn't start working straightaway, I respect the price action and cut it fast."

Chapter 13

Ken Heebner:
Worth Hearing

"Losing money is the least of my troubles. A loss never bothers me after I take it. I forget it overnight." – Jesse Livermore

Name: Kenneth Heebner
Nationality: American
Education: MBA, Harvard University
Occupation: Funds manager

Career

Ken runs Capital Growth Management (CGM), Boston, Massachusetts, which was started in 1990, and part of his funds were performing very well in 2005, until recent huge drawdowns, which should have been controlled more effectively.

Between 2000 and 2010, the fund enjoyed a cumulative growth of 290.2%, when compared to the S&P 500's 16.4%. He is a very good speculator who respects his own hunches and stays away from what he doesn't understand.

Insights

1. Ken was once ranked No. 1 stock picker in USA, but recently his predictions were less accurate and his funds also suffered. Nevertheless, he hasn't lost his love for the markets. Good traders remain passionate about trading in good and bad times.

2. There's one thing that's unsavoury about Ken, especially when compared to Michael Platt. Ken isn't that good at risk management because the losses he suffers when he's wrong are always substantial. For example, CGM Focus lost 48% in 2008 as the global recession hurt commodity prices and a move into beaten-down financial stocks proved premature. You can agree that someone who loses less than 5% in bad trades is better than someone who loses 35% in bad trades. Why would Ken's fund plunge from $10.3 billion to $1.9 billion? It's because he wasn't trading defensively. *It's better to trade not to lose money, instead of trading to make money. That's a defensive form of trading.* Ken himself acknowledged that he'd have done better if he'd been more defensive. However, he always bounces back with time, which is the most important aspect of all – the ability to survive losing streaks and recover losses.

3. Based on his quote at the end of this piece, he doesn't go with the crowd (for they tend to be wrong). He's like a countertrend trader.

4. Trading, for serious traders, should be a passion of a lifetime. At a relatively old age (71), Ken is still passionate about trading. Unlike John Arnold, who retired from active trading at the age of 38, Ken doesn't show any intention to retire. That's the kind of freedom trading offers: you choose when to retire.

5. When you're really good, you'll be a role model to some great traders. One great trader has other role models who're great traders as well; and the other way round.

Conclusion:

James Altucher says something which is true of trading. He says, with art, you have to deal with perfection. Nobody is perfect. For everyone who loves singing, there is always someone who sings better. For everyone who draws, there is always someone who draws better. You can't make art if you are trying to be perfect." This is also true of trading.

This piece ends with a quote from Ken:

"I am completely outside the mainstream. I see the mainstream in the distance."

Chapter 14

Martin Schwartz: He Lost Money For Nine Years Before Making Millions Every Year

"Most traders will quit and stay away from trading after blowing up a few trading accounts. But those with grit will constantly reflect upon their actions and seek to better themselves, which separates the winners from the losers." – Rayner Teo

Name: Martin Schwartz
Year of birth: 1945
Nationality: American
Hobbies: Professional trading and professional horse racing

Career

In 1967, Martin attended Amherst College. He also earned an MBA from Columbia University in 1970. He served in the US Marine Corps Reserves from 1968 to 1973. He also worked as a financial analyst at E. F. Hutton.

He saved about $100,000 and went into full-time trading, buying a seat on the American Stock Exchange. That year, he made a profit of $600,000 and in the following year, he made a profit of $1.2 million. But we need to know that prior to that time, he was a consistent loser in the markets.

In 1984, Martin became famous when he won the US Investing Championship. He has made great wealth from the markets. He authored a book titled *Pit Bull: Lessons from Wall Street's Champion Day Trader*. He loves to go for short-term market fluctuations, and being successful at doing that, he began managing money for other people.

From 2002 till now, Martin Schwartz has been winning in professional horse racing.

Insights

1. Contrary to some people's opinion, it is possible to become a successful trader using technical analysis. When Martin was trading based on fundamentals, he was losing. When he became a technical analyst he earned a fortune. However, there are also successful fundamental analysts. The lesson is that, you shouldn't say something can't work for others just because it isn't working for you.

2. You need to approach the markets as a serious business; those who comply with this fact get paid from those who don't comply.

3. You need to work hard before you can become a profitable trader. There's nothing worth having which comes easily. Hard work is part of your probability of attaining success as a trader.

4. We want to make money, without being necessarily right. We need to master our ego and realize that making money is more important than being right. We make money by cutting our losses, and we lose money by letting them run. Martin Schwartz says that by preserving your capital through the use of stops, you make it possible to wait patiently for a high-probability trade with a low-risk entry-point. One of the great tools of trading is the stop, the point at which you divorce yourself from your emotions and ego and admit that you're wrong.

5. Prepare for each trading day, for it matters a lot. No trades, no profits. You need to pull the trigger before you can hope to make any profits.

Conclusion:

There are traders who have spent many years in the markets without being profitable. Isn't it so frustrating when we keep on losing money in spite of the vast knowledge we have in the markets? We'll be tempted from time to time to conclude that it's impossible to make money trading Forex, yet we won't give up because there is a kind of inner hope that would keep on pushing us to success. We definitely need to be courageous. We shouldn't make things difficult for ourselves when trading. The majority of traders don't want to agree that using difficult trading methods doesn't increase profitability.

This chapter ends with a quote from Martin:

"Trading is a psychological game. Most people think they are playing against the market, but the market doesn't care. You're really playing against yourself."

Chapter 15

Whitney Tilson: Making Profits Effortlessly

"If you like reading biographies on successful people like I do, you'll notice that they all share one driving force. That force drove each of them forward to overcome the obstacles that threatened to stop them in their tracks." – Louise Bedford

Name: Whitney Tilson
Year of birth: 1966
Nationality: American
Occupation: Value investor, author and philanthropist

Career

Whitney Tilson spent his childhood in Nicaragua, Tanzania and Kenya, where his parents have retired. He went to Bing Nursery School, Northfield Mt. Hermon School and Harvard College. In 1994, he also earned an MBA with excellence from Harvard Business School. He was among the top 5% of his class.

Since his parents were both great educators, it's no wonder that their child did well at school.

In 2004, he started Value Investing Congress with John Schwartz. Being highly influenced by great investors, he has co-authored several books including *The Art of Value Investing: How the World's Best Investors Beat the Market* (2013) and *More Mortgage Meltdown: 6 Ways to Profit in These Bad Times* (2009). He has been given copious recognition such as being included in the list of 20 rising stars in 2007 by Institutional Investor, one of five investors in 2006 Power 30, by SmartMoney Magazine, etc.

Although he likes to buy very cheap, he sometimes sells short with a measure of conviction. Like every professional, Whitney isn't always right. During the Google IPO in 2004, he warned against the frenzied buying of the stock. Nevertheless, the stock made huge gains in the following years.

Whitney is involved in various educational, philanthropic and political causes, activities and reforms. He lives in New York, USA.

Insights

1. Great investors aren't always right. Sometimes they do well and sometimes they don't. However, when they aren't right, they just make sure the losses aren't too much. Whitney went through a tough time in 2011 and 2012, but he was able to rebuild gradually and the last few years have been good.

2. Because he is familiar with extreme poverty conditions in Nicaragua, Tanzania and Kenya, Whitney is grateful for the fortune he enjoys. He has a greater appreciation for the incredible good fortune he's had in his life. What a good example from Whitney! Developed countries are full of ungrateful souls who complain about flimsy and ridiculous things. You might deprecate your inability to get shoes until you see someone without legs. No matter your condition, there are others who are worse off than you. You should be thankful for what you've got, no matter what you don't have.

3. Sometimes, one can make money by following a reputable analyst's recommendation. When a market is overextended in a bearish territory owing to dismal fundamental data, it may pose a tempting offer for speculators. The best stock or trading instrument may sometimes become hopelessly weak and that's a great opportunity to buy.

4. "The witches and wizards in my father's household have succeeded in preventing me from succeeding in Forex," one ignorant trader lamented. But the fact is that we make our decisions and are responsible for them. We needn't blame others for our bad trades. Good trades aren't a result of our wisdom, prescience and skill; neither are bad trades a result of ill-luck. Just know the reason why your trades go bad, otherwise you learn very little.

5. The only source of knowledge is experience. Though it's great to look for ways to improve one's timing, it's more rational to respond smartly when timing isn't so perfect

6. A good trader needs to cultivate independent thinking sometimes – that's a necessity. For example, risk control would seem like fun because we'll be able to sleep well, knowing full well that our risk is under control.

7. According to Whitney, the learning process for investors can often be complicated by human nature. Your ability to learn from both successes and failures is a key determinant of how successful an investor you will be.

8. When you have a trading stance that is contrary to the expectation of the majority, you'll need ongoing patience and conviction to stick to that.

9. Never stop learning: otherwise you'll get passed by.

Conclusion:

James Altucher says you shouldn't be sad when you fail and be happy when you succeed. Both are going to happen again and again at every new level. When your excessive worrying goes out of control, then you need to adjust your viewpoint. You need to get help from fellow traders and/or mental trading professionals. When you master your mindset and change your outlook on trading, you will begin to feel you're in control of your fate in the markets, not that the markets are in control of you. Although there will be times when you find it challenging to remain calm, you'll have a better sense of why markets behave the way they do, and you know how to control the risk. Sometimes, the best way out of painful negativity is through it, not around it. That's when you're able to look at open trades rationally, not emotionally.

This chapter is concluded with a quote from Whitney:

"Investors see nothing but sunny skies as far as the eye can see and therefore do not care one iota about risk. They are pursuing returns regardless of risk, and therefore the most speculative companies and investment classes are doing very well."

Chapter 16

Louis Bacon:
A Rare Trading Genius

"…Remember to view setbacks, losses and failures as learning opportunities. All great achievers have made innumerable mistakes and have failed, that is what provided the "experience" and the "education."" – Dr. Woody Johnson

Name: Louis Bacon
Date of birth: 25 July 1953
Nationality: American
Occupation: Hedge Funds Manager

Career

Born in Raleigh, North Carolina, Louis attended Episcopal High School in Alexandria, Virginia. He went to Middlebury College in Vermont, earning a B.A in American literature. In 1981, he got an MBA degree in finance from Columbia Business School.

After getting his MBA, he worked in various capacities at various firms and companies like Bankers Trust, Walter N. Frank & Co, New York Cotton Exchange, and Shearson Lehman Brothers. He founded Remington Trading Partners in 1987 and began to forecast the market crashes and rallies. He traded according to his own forecasts (something that most analysts today don't do) and made huge amount of money from that.

He founded Moore Capital Management LLC in 1989 with the $25,000 he inherited from his family. Needless to say, his ventures became hugely successful. In 2006, Forbes referred to him as the 746th richest person on this planet. In the world's rich list, he took the 736th position in 2011, and he was named the 238th richest American in 2010.

In 2010, Louis Bacon was worth $100,600,000,000.

He has four children from his first marriage. He was remarried in 2007. In November 2007, he bought a $175,000,000-property in Costilla County, Colorado, from the Forbes family. He has also supported political parties and causes.

Insights

1. When did you start trading? Have you faced any challenges? Most trading masters faced losses in the past. Louis started trading with a low interest loan he collected while he was still at Columbia, but he lost money during his first three semesters. He'd to take another loan from his father in order to stay afloat. In the fourth semester, he recovered his losses and made profits. Too many people quit trading after the first or second series of losses

without being aware that they might become very rich in future if they hold out long enough. Someone we call a genius today refused to give up when things seemed hopeless. Louis didn't quit and he is a billionaire today. Do you know the value of a billion dollars in terms of USD?

2. As a speculator you must embrace disorder and chaos. This is what Louis believes. The unpredictability and uncertainties of the trading environment must be embraced and mastered before we can become triumphant in spite of what the market throws at us. We can make money in spite of the fact that the market is uncertain and unpredictable.

3. When you become rich, you will easily engage in other activities in which you are interested. Just like Louis Bacon, you might want to engage in philanthropy. Louis founded the Moore Charitable Foundation (MCF) in 1992, to provide financial support to nonprofit organizations that work to preserve and protect wildlife habitat and improve water systems. He has also contributed millions of dollars to other environmental and conservation organizations, and has thus won well-deserved recognition. In order to emphasize his conservationist views, he says: "I am a conservationist. It is in my DNA... When a profit-seeking company proposes to take citizens' private land away for its own gain, people should stand up for their rights...We are too quickly losing important landscapes in this country to development – and I worry that if we do not act to protect them now, future generations will grow up in a profoundly different world."

Conclusion:

The best way to cut your learning curve and achieve a specific result is to find people who have already achieved what you want and then model their behaviour. Louise Bedford says: Find a mentor, no matter what the cost. A mentor makes a huge difference in your development. Of course, if you have a spare 10 to 20 years up your sleeve to perfect your skills alone, then by all means do so. However, most people want more immediate results. I am where I am because I found good mentors and I followed their advice. Failure can take a great personal cost, and a mentor can help you avoid errors. I don't know how people can begin a business without mentors to help them. (Source: Tradinggame.com.au).

This chapter concludes with a quote from Louis:

"The ability to manage large assets well – it's like being Michael Jordan or winning the gold in the Olympics; it's what you aspire to."

Chapter 17

Sir John Templeton: The Greatest Global Stock Picker of the 20th Century

"A main focus for us is showing traders how to reduce risk with three important tools. The first is the proper use of protective stop orders, the second is proper position size and the last, but maybe most important tool is to keep losses small."
– Sam Seiden

Name: Sir John Templeton
Date of birth: 29 November 1912
Nationality: British, Bahamian (and formerly American)
Occupation: Investor, businessman, researcher, philanthropist
Website: Templeton.org

Career

Sir John Templeton was born in Winchester, Tennessee, USA. He went to Yale University (where he was an assistant business manager for the campus humour magazine). He financed his own education by playing poker – with fine results. He graduated with outstanding performances. As a Rhodes Scholar, he was able to attend Oxford University, bagging an MA in law.

He became a billionaire by being the first person to take advantage of globally diversified mutual funds. He established Templeton Growth Fund, Ltd and was among the first persons to invest in Japan in the 1960s (some of the world's largest and most successful international investment funds).

His website reveals that he took the strategy of "buy low, sell high" to an extreme, picking nations, industries, and companies hitting rock-bottom, what he called "points of maximum pessimism." When war began in Europe in 1939, he borrowed money to buy 100 shares each in 104 companies selling at one dollar per share or less, including 34 companies that were in bankruptcy. Only four turned out to be worthless, and he turned large profits on the others.

Again, he's noted for, during the Depression of the 1930s, buying 100 shares of each NYSE listed company which was then selling for less than $1 a share ($17 today) (104 companies, in 1939), later making many times the money back when USA industry picked up as a result of World War II (as mentioned in Wikipedia).

He has been identified as one of the most generous philanthropists in the history of the world, donating more than $1,000,000,000 to charities. He relinquished his US citizenship in 1964, which enabled him to save $100 million in US income taxes when he sold his international investment fund. That money was used for philanthropy. He had dual naturalized Bahamian and British citizenship and lived in the Bahamas.

He wrote many books, including:

- *Riches for the Mind and Spirit: John Marks Templeton's Treasury of Words to Help, Inspire, and Live By* (2006)

- *Golden Nuggets* (1997)

- *Buying at the Point of Maximum Pessimism: Six Value Investing Trends from China to Oil to Agriculture* (2010)

- *Investing the Templeton Way: The Market Beating Strategies of Value Investing Legendary Bargain Hunter* (2007)

- *Worldwide Laws of Life: 200 Eternal Spiritual Principles* (1998)

As a philanthropist, Sir John established the John Templeton Foundation in 1987, as well as a library, a prize, and a college under the University of Oxford. He donated a sizable amount of his assets to the foundation. That same year, he was created a Knight Bachelor by Queen Elizabeth II for his many philanthropic accomplishments.

A Chartered Financial Analyst (CFA) charter holder, Sir John received AIMR's first award for professional excellence in 1991. Money magazine called him "arguably the greatest global stock picker of the century" in 1999. In 1996, he was inducted into Junior Achievement US Business Hall of Fame, and in 2003, he was awarded the William E. Simon Prize for Philanthropic Leadership. He was named one of Time magazine's 100 Most Influential People in 2007.

Being a lifelong member of the Presbyterian Church, he served in various positions of high responsibilities in the church.

Sir John was married twice and has children. He first married Judith Folk, who died of a motorbike accident in 1951. He then married Irene Reynolds Butler, who died in 1993.

Sir John Templeton died on 8 July 2008, in Nassau, Bahamas, aged 95.

Insights

1. Humility is important to us as traders; and so are good mood, absence of anxiety and discipline.

2. Bull markets arise from pessimistic moods, they thrive on uncertainties and become mature on optimism and confidence, and then they die on euphoria. When the public go mad about a stock, it's time to sell.

3. Avoid the herd mentality. What most people think, believe can't help you. This will remain forever true in the world of trading and investing. Invest at the point of maximum pessimism. Stocks are excellent 'buy' candidates when people don't want to buy them because they're terrible. Please read Sir John's career above again. Think about how he made his money. He invested in Japan when most people thought that idea was crazy. He sold his stocks when the public showed excessive confidence in them, when values and expectations were high. There are investment opportunities all over the world, not in the US alone. Sir John himself said: "The other boys at Yale came from wealthy families, and none of them were investing outside the United States, and I thought, 'That is very egotistical. Why be so short-sighted or near-sighted as to focus only on America? Shouldn't you be more open-minded?'"

4. If you want to have a better performance than the crowd, you must do things differently from the crowd. Since most traders lose, you need to do what most traders don't do to be successful.

5. It's possible to make money solely from fundamental analysis (just as it's possible to make money solely from technical analysis). Sir John didn't do technical systems; he based his investment decisions solely on fundamentals. Those using technical analyses only shouldn't criticize those using fundamentals only: and vice

versa. Any trading approach is good, no matter how weird, as long as it makes money.

6. Sir John – though a generous giver – never spent too much money on himself. Uninterested in consumerism, he drove his own car, never flew first class and lived year-round in the Bahamas. Being rich doesn't necessarily mean we should live an extremely flamboyant, ostentatious, and expensive life. Warren Buffet is another good example.

7. Sir John, who was also interested in spiritual matters, said: "We are trying to persuade people that no human has yet grasped 1% of what can be known about spiritual realities. So we are encouraging people to start using the same methods of science that have been so productive in other areas, in order to discover spiritual realities."

Conclusion:

James Altucher quotes Marilyn Monroe as saying "Imperfection is beauty, madness is genius and it's better to be absolutely ridiculous than absolutely boring." He also says you should be embarrassed by what you do. Give yourself permission to be imperfect. Out of that messy soup of shame and imperfection will come art.' No matter how many periods of discouragement you face, know that a good state of the mind, a sensible strategy and lack of expectations are what you will ultimately need to succeed. That's the only method for survival in the world of uncertainties.

This chapter concludes with a quote from Sir John:

"In my 45-year career as an investment counselor, humility did show me the need for worldwide diversification to reduce risk. That career did help me to become more and more humble because statistics showed that when I advised a client to buy one stock to replace another, about one-third of the time the client would have done better to ignore my advice. In other endeavors, humility about how little I know has encouraged me to listen more carefully and more wisely."

Chapter 18

Michael Steinhardt:
Wall Street's Greatest Trader?

"The trading game is not won in the strategy one selects. The trading game is won in the mind." – DbPhoenix (Source: Trade2win.com)

Name: Michael Steinhardt
Date of birth: 7 December 1940
Nationality: American
Occupation: Funds Manager and philanthropy

Career

Michael was born to an American Jewish family. His father was a notorious gambler who was his son's first client. He provided the seed money for Michael to start his investment career.

Michael Steinhardt attended the University of Pennsylvania. After graduating in 1960, he worked for a brokerage firm. He started his own hedge fund in 1967, with some partners. One source reports that his fund averaged an annualized return for its clients of 24.5%, after a 1% management fee and a "performance fee" of 15% (early in his career, later 20%) of all annual gains, realized and unrealized, nearly triple the annualized performance of the S&P 500 Index over the same timeframe.

Because of his continuous success in the markets, Michael was investigated for allegedly trying to manipulate the short-term Treasury Note market, because his firm personally made $600 million from trading Treasury. The case was settled after a fine of $70 million was paid.

His fund sustained a loss in 1994 but enjoyed good returns in 1995. This shows that even great speculators can't always win. But unlike short-sighted speculators, they don't quit because they know things will soon turn out in their favour.

Michael closed his fund in 1995 and returned the capital to his clients. He came out extremely affluent and liquid.

In 2004, he came out of retirement and started working for WisdomTree Investments (formerly known as Index Development Partners). He is chairman of that company; whose worth increases by about 10% per month, with $18.3 billion under management. The company suffered some losses in 2007 and 2008 as a result of the credit crunch that ravaged the financial world. Nevertheless, the company has recovered and moved ahead.

Because of his Jewish ethnicity, Michael Steinhardt donates generously to several Jewish causes, programs and events he believes in. He also donates generously to other political, academic and humanitarian causes.

Michael was married in 1967 and has three children. In 2001, he released an autobiography titled: *No Bull: My Life in and out of Markets*.

Insights

1. Michael mastered several markets instead of just one. He traded stocks, currencies, bonds and options, using small and large timeframes. He is a trend-follower. You too can master more than one investment vehicle.

2. According to Michael, you should make all your mistakes early in life. The more tough lessons you learn early on, the fewer errors you make later. Always make your living doing something you enjoy.

3. You need to study the markets and gather lots of information so that you can sense major shifts in the trend. You can't know everything, however. So you need to make your trading decisions with incomplete information. You will never have all the information you need. What matters is what you do with the information you have.

4. Always trust your intuition – although that doesn't mean you will always be right. When you are eventually right, the thought of having made a profit will be very satisfying.

5. Before your risk your money, make sure the reward is high enough to justify the time and effort you put into the investment decision.

6. Michael Steinhardt used fundamentals when trading, although his positions were short-term. He did an enormous amount of trading, not necessarily just for profit, but also because it opens up

other opportunities. He got a chance to be involved with a lot of things. Trading is a catalyst.

Conclusion:

"There's no way to know in advance if a business idea is a good one. For instance, Google started around 1996 but didn't make a dime of money until around 2001," says James Altucher. He also says... don't be afraid to test, fail, test, fail, try again, repeat, improve, test, fail again, and keep improving. The way to keep improving? Keep coming up with ideas for your business and for other new businesses. How true these statements are when it comes to trading!

This chapter concludes with a quote from Michael Steinhardt:

"One dollar invested with me in 1967 would have been worth $481 on the day I closed the firm in 1995, versus $19 if it had been invested in a Standard & Poor's index fund."

Chapter 19

Bill Miller:
One of the Greatest
Money Managers

"Just as picking up a five iron does not make you Tiger Woods, opening a brokerage account and sitting in front of a computer screen does not make you Peter Lynch or Warren Buffett. That is something you must work for, and it takes time and practice. What is important is that you learn how to practice correctly." – Mark Minervini

Name: Bill Miller
Year of birth: 1950
Nationality: American
Occupation: Portfolios manager

Career

Bill Miller went to Washington and Lee University, graduating in 1972 (BSc Economics). Following that, he worked as a military intelligence officer, also pursuing graduate studies in the PhD program at the Johns Hopkins University.

He was a treasurer of the J.E. Baker Company, a major manufacturer of products for the steel and cement industries. In 1981, he started working at Legg Mason. He was designated a CFA in 1986.

Bill's fund increased from $750,000,000 in 1990 to more than $20,000,000,000 in 2006.

In 2002, Janet Lowe wrote a book about him, titled *The Man Who Beats The S&P: Investing With Bill Miller.*

Bill performed so well that he and his team received much praise for their achievements and their unique trading approaches. According to Wikipedia, he was ranked among the top 30 most influential people in investing when he was named a member of the "Power 30" by SmartMoney. He was also named by Money magazine as "the Greatest Money Manager of the 1990s" and named Morningstar's 1998 "Domestic Equity Manager of the Year." In 1999, he was selected as the "Fund Manager of the Decade" by Morningstar.com. Also in 1999, Barron's named him to its All-Century Investment Team and BusinessWeek called him one of the "Heroes of Value Investing."

Bill is currently the portfolio manager of the Legg Mason Opportunity Trust (Mutual fund: LMOPX) mutual funds, run by Miller through Legg Mason subsidiary LMM. Before that, he was the chairman and chief investment officer at of Legg Mason Capital Management, now a part of ClearBridge.

Insights

1. It's quite possible to outperform the markets for a long period of time. Bill Miller beat the S&P 500 index for 15 consecutive years (1991 to 2005). This is one of the longest winning streaks of a trading career. Constantly making market beating returns is considered to be very unlikely according to the efficient market hypothesis, but it's possible. So in your career, you can defy the conventional theory and rise beyond obstacles.

2. Information simply shows what's happened while value shows what may happen. It will be in your best interest to think about the big picture.

3. Bill says certainty belongs to mathematics, not to markets, and anyone who awaits clarity, visibility or the diminution of uncertainty pays a high price for a chimera... It's the nature of financial markets to be subject to sharp price fluctuations, to be buffeted by events, and often to be emotionally trying. Successful investing involves the disciplined and patient execution of a long-term strategy, especially when it's emotionally difficult. That's usually the time the opportunities are the greatest.

4. Most money managers take positions as they swing to their opposites. Those swings can have wide arcs, and unsustainable trends can sometimes persist beyond the ability of one to endure. This explains why speculators sell their positions in over-extended bear markets, for they can't continue enduring the pain of losing. When bull markets become over-extended, speculators are glad to go in fully, thinking that the bullish trend will continue in spite of the fact that things look overbought.

5. Flying in the face of conventional trading wisdom, Bill explains what value investing really means to him: "We are value investors because we are persuaded of the logic of buying shares of

businesses when others want to sell them, and we understand that lower prices today mean higher future rates of return, and high prices today mean lower future rates of return."

6. The real secrets behind Bill's super performance (which is very difficult to copy) is that he spent many years studying independent super achievers, and along the way he has become one of the super achievers.

Conclusion:

Louise Bedford of Tradinggame.com.au once said that you'd better start seeking out people who are making a lot more money than you are. You will naturally rise to the occasion and start moving forward. Your thinking will change. Your habits will change. Traders who make a million plus per year think differently and act differently to those making 100K per year. The fact is, if your mates are telling you 100K per year is fantastic, but your goal is to get to 500K a year... then you'd better find another group. There are those who imagine the future; there are those who create the future. Permanent victory is easier when the mission is clear. Here, we are dedicated to making our trading career a success story.

This chapter concludes with quotes from Bill:

"The market does reflect the available information, as the professors tell us. But just as the funhouse mirrors don't always accurately reflect your weight, the markets don't always accurately reflect that information. Usually they are too pessimistic when it's bad, and too optimistic when it's good."

"What we try to do is take advantage of errors others make, usually because they are too short-term oriented, or they react to dramatic events, or they overestimate the impact of events, and so on."

Chapter 20

James Tisch:
Moving Ahead
of Warren Buffet

"Books are great mentors, but where else can you learn? By standing on the shoulders of giants. When it comes to making money, here is the million dollar secret... follow someone smarter than you..." – James Altucher

Name: James Tisch
Date of birth: 2 January 1953
Nationality: American
Occupation: Investor and businessman

Career

James, who is of Jewish ethnicity, was born in Southampton, New York, USA.

His father was co-chair of Loews Corporation, plus his brother Preston Tisch. He went to Cornell University and later got his MBA from the Wharton School of the University of Pennsylvania.

James has held prestigious positions, including having a seat in the directorate of the Federal Reserve Bank of New York. He has been the CEO of Loews Corporation since 1999.

One thing special about him is that, in terms of percentage, his investments have outperformed Warren Buffet's.

He is married to Merryl and has three children. James has a mansion which is about 8,000 square feet in Southampton, New York. James is an avid philanthropist, and a supporter of certain politicians. He and his wife donated $40 million to found a cancer research institute, named after them.

Insights

1. Transparency matters in business success. If you claim you are good at trading/investing, then you must make your audited track record known.

2. Transparency leads to credibility. Credibility leads to more and more success. Simply look for ways to make your career credible. Success will then be very easy.

3. James has been investing for many years. He really is a veteran of the markets. Successful trading needs a commitment of a lifetime – just like a successful marriage. Commitment is what you need to realize your dreams, not mere interest.

4. If you're good enough, you can outperform the bigwigs. This means you can gain more than they can, in terms of percentage,

though their portfolios may be bigger than yours. You can make 40% per annum on a $100,000 portfolio: whereas someone who's managing $10 million could only make 6% per annum. Can you see the difference? As mentioned earlier, one thing special about James is that, in terms of percentage, his investments have outperformed Warren Buffet's. He may not be as rich as Warren, but he outperforms him in terms of percentage gains. Since 2000, James has grown by almost 400% while Warren has grown by only 100%.

Conclusion:

Do you think you're a god who can predict the markets? Can you predict football matches with utmost certainty, even before the matches start? If you could do that, would you do that for other types of sports? Can you predict exactly when you will die or when a healthy person will die? Why do you still think the future can be predicted? Why do you still think you can predict the markets? People get frustrated only because they think they can predict the markets (but they can't, in reality). When you agree that it's unrealistic to think that you can predict the market with whatever tools you may have, then you'll find a solution to your trading problems. You'll develop a system that enables you to make money without predicting the markets. James Tisch was able to attain good performances because he has formulas that make him victorious while not being able to know the future.

This chapter is concluded by the quote below:

"Event-driven trading can be very lucrative." – Dr. Adrian Manz

Conclusion

I'd like to conclude this book with *"Three questions traders would like to ask right now."*

Why is trading so difficult?

Answer: What makes trading appear very difficult is the fact that the market can never be predicted. When we predict, we're sometimes wrong or right. However, having an impression that the market can be predicted is the single most important reason why most traders end getting frustrated. No matter the analytical method you use (Monte Carlo, Neural Networks, Horology, robots, Gann, news, Ichimoku, etc), you can't predict the future. Your frustration will continue as long as you think you can predict the market. Once you admit you can't do this, your frustration ends, because you've aligned yourself with the reality in the market.

What benefit can I get from trading?

Answer: Freedom. Freedom is everything. You master your financial destiny, growing richer and richer gradually. Very soon, you'll realize that trading is the best vehicle for financial freedom; plus the greatest game on earth. Sadly, many people don't believe this fact.

How can I experience permanent success in the markets?

Answer: You will attain permanent success once you devise a way to make money in the market without being able to predict the market – without knowing what the market will do next. This kind of strategy isn't hard to devise. You'll then see each new trade as a potential loser until you're proven otherwise. This mindset will enable you to activate stops and use a small position size. You'll know trading is simply a game of probability and with a good RRR, the odds will eventually come in your favour. This is what's called positive expectancy. With this simple approach, you'll no longer see trading as difficult. More importantly, you will attain permanent success without the ability to know the future, which begins from your mind.

About the Author

Azeez Mustapha is a trading professional, funds manager, an InstaForex official analyst, a blogger at ADVFN.com, and a freelance author for trading magazines. He works as a trading signals provider at various websites and his numerous articles are posted on many websites such as:www.ituglobalforex.blogspot.com.

Contact: azeez.mustapha@analytics.instaforex.com.

Azeez has published three previous books with ADVFN Books: *Learn From the Generals of the Markets*, *What Super Traders Don't Want You to Know* and *Super Trading Strategies*. Turn over for more details of these titles.

Also by Azeez Mustapha

Super Trading Strategies

If you want to be a success trading on the Forex markets, you need to know what you are doing. Learning by trial and error can be expensive and one wrong move could wipe you out. You need help to know what strategies work and how they should be used.

Super Trading Strategies gives you a set of concrete and easy-to-use trading strategies that will help you on your way to making money. They all work on the Forex markets, and some are also applicable to the stock and futures markets.

These super trading strategies include short-term, long-term, swing and positions trading strategies. Some are ideal for part-time traders and some for full-time traders.

Each strategy is explained in detail with examples of how they can be used and charts illustrating the currency movements to which they apply. At the end of each chapter, a strategy snapshot summarises what you have learned.

Written by an experienced Forex trader who is also a journalist and writer, *Super Trading Strategies* will help you win the battles of the Forex markets.

The strategies were previously published in TRADERS' magazine.

Available in paperback and for the Kindle.

What Super Traders Don't Want You to Know

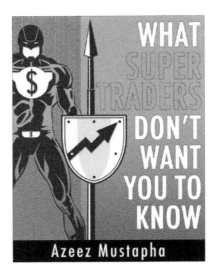

If you want to succeed as a trader, you need to learn the necessary skills.

Risk your money on the markets without knowing what you are doing, and you could lose it all. Just like any other profession, to be a trader requires you to learn from the experts.

What Super Traders Don't Want You To Know profiles twenty-two renowned super traders from around the world, great traders who know what it takes to be successful in the markets. In this follow up to his previous book *Learn From the Generals of the Markets*, Azeez Mustapha gives an overview of their careers and explains what lessons can be drawn from their success.

You can apply their methods and techniques to your own trading, and gain the expertise you need to improve your prospects.

This essential guide could start you on the path to becoming a super trader.

Available in paperback and for the Kindle.

Learn From the Generals of the Market

If you want to win on the trading battlefield, you need the right ammunition.

Trading is like any other profession: to succeed, you need to arm yourself with the necessary skills. Enter the arena without knowing what you are doing, and you are sure to lose your money.

You need help from the experts.

Learn From the Generals of the Markets profiles twenty renowned super traders from around the world, great traders who know what it takes to be successful in the markets. The book gives an overview of their careers and explains what lessons can be drawn from their success, so you can apply their methods and techniques to your own trading. It will help you gain the expertise you need to improve your prospects.

This essential guide should be part of every trader's armament.

Available in paperback and for the Kindle.

More Books from ADVFN

Trade Financial Markets Like The Pros

by Simon Watkins

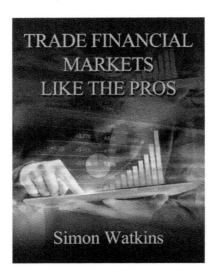

There has never been a more difficult time to make money from trading the markets than now. All of the long-standing foundation stones of the global financial system are in a state of flux: engines of growth, monetary policies and the correlation dynamics between asset classes.

Additionally, each of the four core regional growth engines around the world – the US, the Eurozone, China and Japan – face their own sets of problems, undermining the historic relationships between stocks, bonds and currencies even further.

Given this backdrop, it is more important than ever that traders manage and exploit the few remaining factors in global markets that hold good. This is what this book is about: knowing what these are, exploiting them and banking the profits in a risk/reward efficient manner.

Fully illustrated with detailed charts, *Trade Financial Markets Like The Pros* covers how to balance risk against reward, how to search out correlations between asset classes that offer trading opportunities, and the major factors that could continue to twist financial markets into wildly contradictory modes. It also gives a refresher course in technical analysis and the full range of hedging techniques, including options, to offset possible losses.

Whether you are an experienced trader or just starting out, the information in this book offers you strategies to become one of the winners in the financial markets, and to avoid risking catastrophic losses.

Available in paperback and for the Kindle.

The Great Oil Price Fixes And How To Trade Them

by Simon Watkins

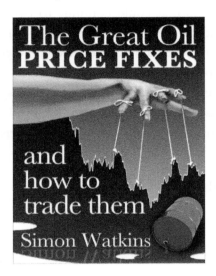

The oil market has been manipulated to an extremely high degree for decades, both overtly and covertly, and given its enduring geopolitical importance that is likely to continue.

Traders need to understand the essential dynamics that drive the global oil market, offering as it does unparalleled opportunities to make returns over and above those of other markets. The oil market is also an essential part of trading FX, equities, bonds and other commodities.

Simon Watkins' book *The Great Oil Price Fixes And How To Trade Them* offers you the knowledge you need. It covers the history of the market, gives you an understanding of the players in the oil game, and provides a solid grounding in the market-specific trading nuances required in this particular field.

The essential elements of the general trading methodology, strategies and tactics that underpin top professional traders are covered with reference to how they can be used to trade in the oil market.

Available in paperback and for the Kindle.

18 Smart Ways to Improve Your Trading

by Maria Psarra

Any trader or investor that says they have never lost money in the markets is too young, too stupid, too inexperienced, or just plain lying to you. Everyone makes mistakes, particularly when starting out as a trader. It's part of the learning curve.

What matters is that you learn from your mistakes. Even better, learn from the mistakes others have made to avoid making them yourself.

18 Smart Ways to Improve Your Trading explains some of the common mistakes traders make and the routines that winning traders use to avoid those errors. The author draws on her many years' experience of trading, both on institutional proprietary trading desks and for herself, and the knowledge she has gained advising professional clients.

In this book she shares her expertise with you. The *18 Smart Ways* include the habits that separate winning traders from losing ones, the secrets to profitable trading and how to deal with the emotional hiccups that cause you to lose in the markets.

If you absorb these lessons then they should make you a better investor or trader.

Originally published as articles in Master Investor magazine.

Available in paperback and for the Kindle.

101 Charts for Trading Success

by Zak Mir

Using insider knowledge to reveal the tricks of the trade, Zak Mir's *101 Charts for Trading Success* explains the most complex set ups in the stock market.

Providing a clear way of predicting price action, charting is a way of making money by delivering high probability percentage trades, whilst removing the need to trawl through company accounts and financial ratios.

Illustrated with easy to understand charts this is the accessible, essential guide on how to read, understand and use charts, to buy and sell stocks. *101 Charts* is a must for all future investment millionaires.

Available in paperback and for the Kindle.

The Game in Wall Street

by Hoyle and Clem Chambers

As the new century dawned, Wall Street was a game and the stock market was fixed. Ordinary investors were fleeced by big institutions that manipulated the markets to their own advantage and they had no comeback.

The Game in Wall Street shows the ways that the titans of rampant capitalism operated to make money from any source they could control. Their accumulated funds gave the titans enormous power over the market and allowed them to ensure they won the game.

Traders joining the game without knowing the rules are on a road to ruin. It's like gambling without knowing the rules and with no idea of the odds.

The Game in Wall Street sets out in detail exactly how this market manipulation works and shows how to ride the price movements and make a profit.

And guess what? The rules of the game haven't changed since the book was first published in 1898. You can apply the same strategies in your own investing and avoid losing your shirt by gambling against the professionals.

Illustrated with the very first stock charts ever published, the book contains a new preface and a conclusion by stock market guru Clem Chambers which put the text in the context of how Wall Street operates today.

Available in paperback and for the Kindle.

For more information, go to the ADVFN Books website at www.advfnbooks.com.

ADVFN BOOKS

Lightning Source UK Ltd.
Milton Keynes UK
UKOW06f1823070417
298629UK00008B/137/P

9 781908 756879